Growing Readers

New Hanover County Public Library

Purchased with
New Hanover County Partnership for Children
and SmartStart Funds

Let's Read About Our Bodies

Hair

by Cynthia Klingel* and Robert B. Noyed
photographs by Gregg Andersen

*Amoroso is preferred name

Reading consultant: Cecilia Minden-Cupp, Ph.D.,
Adjunct Professor, College of Continuing and Professional Studies, University of Virginia

For a free color catalog describing Weekly Reader® Early Learning Library's list of high-quality books, call 1-800-542-2595 or fax your request to (414) 332-3567.

Library of Congress Cataloging-in-Publication Data

Klingel, Cynthia.
   Hair / by Cynthia Klingel and Robert B. Noyed.
      p. cm. — (Let's read about our bodies)
   Includes bibliographical references and index.
   Summary: An introduction to hair, its characteristics, and how to take care of it.
   ISBN 0-8368-3065-2 (lib. bdg.)
   ISBN 0-8368-3154-3 (softcover)
   1. Hair—Juvenile literature. [1. Hair.] I. Noyed, Robert B. II. Title.
   QP88.3.K553   2002
   611'.78—dc21   2001055056

This edition first published in 2002 by
Weekly Reader® Early Learning Library
330 West Olive Street, Suite 100
Milwaukee, WI 53212 USA

An Editorial Directions book
Editors: E. Russell Primm and Emily Dolbear
Art direction, design, and page production: The Design Lab
Photographer: Gregg Andersen
Weekly Reader® Early Learning Library art direction: Tammy Gruenewald
Weekly Reader® Early Learning Library production: Susan Ashley

Printed in the United States of America

1 2 3 4 5 6 7 8 9 06 05 04 03 02

Note to Educators and Parents

As a Reading Specialist I know that books for young children should engage their interest, impart useful information, and motivate them to want to learn more.

Let's Read About Our Bodies is a new series of books designed to help children understand the value of good health and taking care of their bodies.

A young child's active mind is engaged by the carefully chosen subjects. The imaginative text works to build young vocabularies. The short, repetitive sentences help children stay focused as they develop their own relationship with reading. The bright, colorful photographs of children enjoying good health habits complement the text with their simplicity and both entertain and encourage young children to want to learn — and read — more.

These books are designed to be used by adults as "read-to" books to share with children to encourage early literacy in the home, school, and library. They are also suitable for more advanced young readers to enjoy on their own.

— Cecilia Minden-Cupp, Ph.D.,
Adjunct Professor, College of Continuing and
Professional Studies, University of Virginia

This is my hair.
It is on the top
of my head.

Hair can be many colors.

Hair can be long or short.

Some hair is curly.
Some hair is not.

Sometimes I like to have my hair cut.

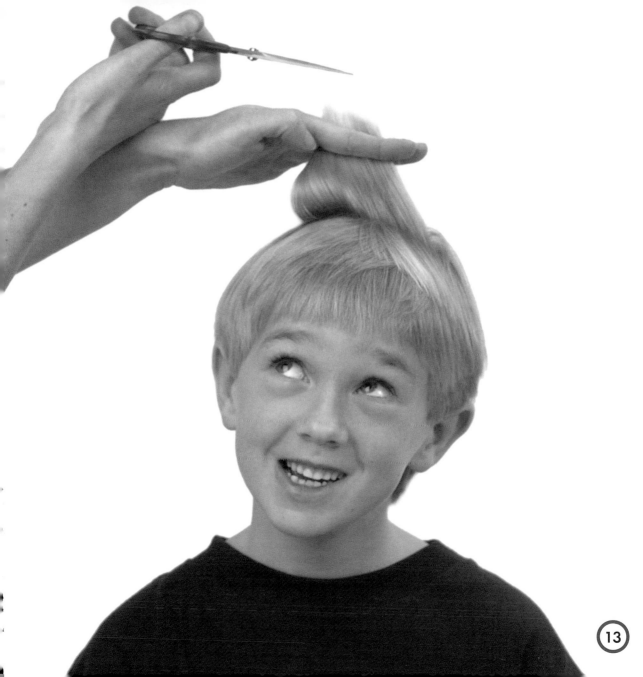

13

I keep my hair neat. I use a brush and comb.

Sometimes I like to wear things in my hair.

I wash my hair to keep it clean.

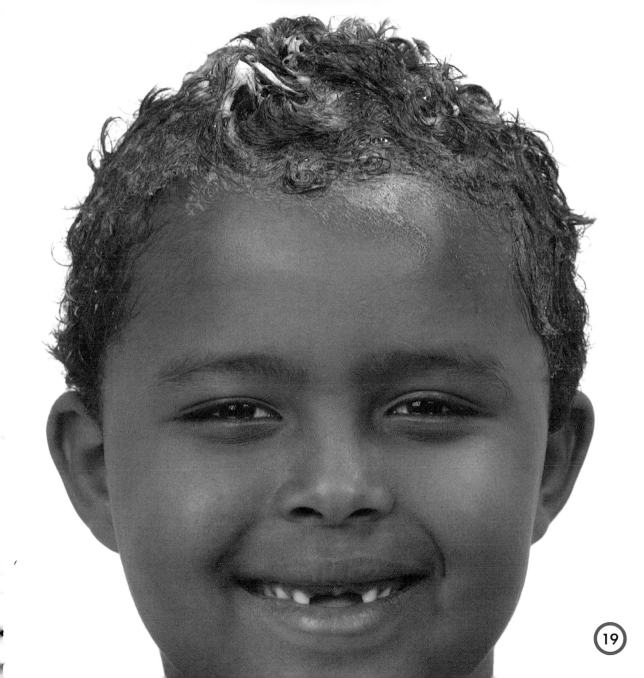

Uh-oh. Now my hair is crazy!

Glossary

clean—to be free from dirt

comb—a flat tool with a row of teeth used to make your hair neat

crazy—wild or uncontrolled

curly—bending or twisting in a spiral shape

neat—clean and orderly

For More Information

Fiction Books

Munsch, Robert N. *Aaron's Hair*. New York: Scholastic, 2000.

Palatini, Margie. *Bedhead*. New York: Simon & Schuster, 2000.

Nonfiction Books

Kroll, Virginia L. *Hats Off to Hair!* Watertown, Mass.: Charlesbridge Publishing, 1995.

Sandeman, Anna. *Skin, Teeth, & Hair*. Brookfield, Conn.: Copper Beech Books, 1996.

Web Sites

Say Hello to Hair and Nails!

kidshealth.org/kid/body/hair_nailNsw.html

For more information about your hair

Index

brushes, 14

cleaning, 18

colors, 6

combs, 14

curly, 10

haircuts, 12

head, 4

length, 8

neatness, 14

About the Authors

Cynthia Klingel has worked as a high school English teacher and an elementary school teacher. She is currently the curriculum director for a Minnesota school district. Cynthia Klingel lives with her family in Mankato, Minnesota.

Robert B. Noyed started his career as a newspaper reporter. Since then, he has worked in school communications and public relations at the state and national level. Robert B. Noyed lives with his family in Brooklyn Center, Minnesota.

5/02